Odysseus in Absaroka

Odysseus in Absaroka

Poems by

John David Muth

Kelsay Books

ISBN: 978-1-947465-68-8

Kelsay Books
Aldrich Press
www.kelsaybooks.com

For Amy and Corinne

Acknowledgements

Anti-Heroin Chic: "Nostalgia in Baggage Claim"

Better Than Starbucks!: "Benadryl and Whiskey"

Eunoia Review: "The Man from Chechnya"

Exit 13 Magazine: "First Night at a Mountain Ranch"

Rat's Ass Review: "Unconscious in Wyoming"

Verse-Virtual: "A Small Mechanical Failure," "Betty Grable was Probably Here," "Flying the Malevolent Skies," and "Imagining Waterfalls"

Contents

Part I: Her Tight White Blouse Made Me Do It

Her Tight White Blouse Made Me Do It

I walk into a travel agency.
A man with a short mustache
wearing a blue blazer with gold buttons
motions me over.
His handshake is sweaty and enthusiastic.

I tell him I want a vacation,
a nice, quiet place
far away from my students
and the gridlock hell of central New Jersey,
maybe a beach on the Adriatic
or a serene cruise to Iceland.

He tells me cruises are for retirees
and metro-sexual bank managers.
The Adriatic is a cesspool.
I need something vigorous
something to sweat out the toxins.
Riffling through a desk drawer
he pulls out a brochure
holds it at eye level
but doesn't allow me to take it.

Hike Western Wyoming's Absaroka Mountain Range
Enjoy beautiful scenery and wildlife
Make friendships that will last a lifetime.

Sensing my reluctance
he calls over his assistant:
a well-endowed twenty-something
with a tight white blouse
and black mini skirt.

He asks her what she thinks about mountain hiking.
She pauses,
arches her back to make her breasts look larger
tosses her raven hair
says she thinks rugged guys are sexy.
She'd break up with her boyfriend
to date a mountain hiker.

Indigestion, Indecision, and Resignation

I lie on my bed
the strength to pack for my hiking trip
drained by a bout of indigestion.
My duffel bag overflows like a volcano
with hiking poles and bug spray
moleskin and anti-microbial underwear.
Will it get cold enough for a sweater?
Should I bring band-aids for blisters?
Do I really need gaiters?
They seem so superfluous.

The couple next door is arguing.
Today, she is complaining about
his choice of restaurants.
Boyfriends should not take girlfriends
to a German restaurant
for their six-month dating anniversary.
Sauerbraten and spaetzle are not romantic.
She should have picked the place
even though she told him
anything was good
as long as they were together.

Cheap Chinese food
kicks and screams
through my digestive system.
Through the pain,
I listen for his response
but there is nothing.
I imagine him regretting
the one who got away
or having a light-hearted daydream

of assault and murder
where everyone applauds the bloody deed
even the police and her parents.

Cannibalism Du Jour

My exasperated taxi driver
talks on his phone
in an incomprehensible language
steers with his knees
so he can use his hands for emphasis.

He pauses from his conversation
to tell me in almost perfect English:
We'll be there in about ten minutes.
I turn on the light in my wristwatch.
The time reads 4:05 a.m.
Twenty minutes would be more accurate.

A hornet's nest of aircraft comes into view.
We are almost there:
Newark Liberty International Airport
my rocket to Wyoming
and a week of hiking
in the Absaroka Mountains
far away from the tourist traps
of Yellowstone and Jackson Hole.

A knight's gauntlet opens and closes
inside my stomach.
My blood pressure starts to rise
as I recall the ordeal of flying
anticipating the frustration
dreading the impediments.

My driver drops me off
still talking on the phone
and as the terminal doors slide open
I wonder if the Donner Party
ever imagined
when they first left Missouri
they'd be stranded in the snow
eating one another
a hundred miles from their destination.

Part II: Flying the Malevolent Skies

Newark, New Jersey to Jackson Hole, Wyoming

Scheduled Departure Time: 6:09 a.m. (EST)

Actual Departure Time: 9:01 a.m. (EST)

Benadryl and Whiskey

We stand for hours
in the baggage check section
silent and forlorn
like ancient Egyptian slaves
sealed into a pharaoh's tomb
waiting to die from starvation.

Sometimes, there is movement
the shuffling of feet
a stanchion rattling
from the careless brush of a purse.
The self check-in kiosks are all down.
Slowly moving airport employees
sip Benadryl and whiskey
from large metal cups
as they scribble signatures
on boarding passes
stifle laughs as the elderly
try to lift their suitcases onto the scales.

I give my boarding pass
to a frowning man
balding and bespectacled
put my luggage on the scale.
He tells me there is an extra charge
for bags over 50 pounds.
The scale reads 36.5 pounds
until he puts his foot on the pressure plate
and the weight jumps to 51.3.
When I open my mouth to protest
he says it is entirely possible
they will find a firearm
hidden in my shaving kit.

Spike Implants as Deadly Weapons

Waiting in line at the airport
she takes out her nose ring
tongue piercing
the navel ring that anchors her belly chain
the twenty-two earrings
on each earlobe
and the sterling silver tooth grill
her boyfriend bought her
for their six-month anniversary.

But when she walks through the metal detector
the sirens scream
and the crowd around her
falls to the ground
covers their heads.
TSA officers shout into walkie-talkies.

I imagine her sitting
in the airport security office
surrounded by armed guards
the sergeant in charge says a note
from her cosmetic surgeon
is insufficient proof
she is not a terrorist.
The spikes lining her thoracic spine
can be considered deadly weapons.

FBI agents enter the room.
When she stands,
her spike implants shred
the foam rubber cushion of the chair.

The Body Scanner

A woman stands in front
of a body scanner
5'8" and slender
blue-eyed, blonde, beautiful.
Back arched
hands above her head
her hairline mists with perspiration.
She's been holding this position
for almost five minutes.

Airport security officers
gather around the screen
holding cups of coffee
eyes transfixed
nudging one another.

She asks if the machine
can see her naked
wants to know when they'll be done.
An officer says it takes time to scan
but the image of her body will be indistinct.
He snaps a picture with his phone.

Another woman looks at her watch
stomps her foot in anger
walks through the security gate
without being scanned.
None of the guards notice.

Misogyny in an Airport Bar

A soft-voiced announcer
tells us our flight will be delayed
for at least several hours.
No explanation is given.

The dawn sun leers through the windows
of the airport lounge.
People lie on the floor
backpacks for pillows
sleep slumped over chairs
weakly pace back and forth
like an apocalyptic cult
in the last throes of suicide.

Fighting frustration, I go to the bar
order a glass of beer.
Two men sitting next to me
talk about their luck with online dating.

The shorter man tells his friend
women are like Matryoshka Dolls,
the more layers he pops off
the less interesting and unique they become.
His last girlfriend was little more
than two dots for eyes and a wisp of hair.

The bearded guy says
women in their mid-40's are the easiest to bed.
They are desperate to please
and long for marriage
but he'll never marry again.
Four times is enough.

Their callousness appeals to me,
hurt and slighted many times
but never enjoying comeuppance.
I peer into my dripping glass.
The smile of my yellow reflection
starts to make me nauseous.

The Man from Chechnya

He reads a magazine
during the safety lecture
while the flight attendant
points out the exits on the plane.

She leers at him
says they will not take off
until everyone is paying attention.
He tells her he has flown a thousand times
knows the oxygen mask descends
when the cabin loses pressure,
knows how to use the life jacket
should they splash down over Nebraska.
He even knows the number
of a very good dentist
who might repair the ivory Stonehenge
she calls teeth.

The flight attendant storms down the aisle
awakens the air marshal from his nap
said she heard the man in seat 23C mutter
something in Arabic.
It sounded like the word, "bomb."
Questioned by the marshal
the man tries to explain he is a Presbyterian
born in Nevada
a true-blue American.
His parents left Czechoslovakia
to escape from Communist oppression.
The marshal thought he said Chechnya
so he is escorted off the plane
and probably put on the No-Fly List.

Fred Goes on Vacation

The passenger in front of me
reclines his seat all the way
crushes my bag of potato chips
pins my hands between the seat back
and the tray table.

He lifts his chin to see me upside-down
my frown now a smile
says his name is Fred.
He and the wife are going to Dallas
for a vacation.

Before I can ask him to get off my hands,
he starts to chat:
Do you remember the days
when airlines served free meals
asked if you wanted a pillow
treated you like a person?
Why don't they do that anymore?

The teenage boy to my right
looks at me quizzically.
I sadly nod, as if to say:
Yes. We were treated like humans once,
before the dark times,
before the days of total exploitation.

The boy lowers his head.
I do the same
look at Fred's liver-spotted forehead
crease with laughter.
He's now watching the in-flight movie:
Snakes on a Plane.

Terminal Hopping and Barbequed Beef

The Dallas Airport
is a five-headed hydra
that taunts me during my layover.

I ride the monorail
connecting the terminals
eating a twenty-dollar
handcrafted barbeque beef
and cayenne provolone sandwich
served with arugula on an asiago bun.
The cashier did not answer me
when I asked what handcrafted meant
and whether it was possible
to make a sandwich without hands.

The monorail moves hesitantly
and the track shudders
like the synapses of a college student
who failed theater appreciation.
My flight landed at terminal A.
The connecting flight was terminal B
but when I got to B
the arrival screen changed to terminal E.
Then, it changed to C
and for nearly an hour I played
this toy piano melody
until my plane finally arrived.

I shuffle quickly to the gate
carrying a bag spotted with grease
intestines churning from old roast beef.
An old man in a cowboy hat

notices the logo on the bag
and my mild green complexion,
mutters as I pass by:
You eat that in the barbeque capital of the world, son?
I hope you learned your lesson.

Flying the Malevolent Skies

Flight attendant
evil winged waitress
rams her beverage cart
into my knee
chuckles an apology
tosses a bag of almonds on my groin
and I recall the sensitivity of gonads.

The contortionist seated to my right
gives me a scowl
itches her cerebellum
with the back of her left heel
tells me leg room is for sissies.

But even though my arrival time
has been delayed for many hours,
even though a bearded TSA officer
patted me down a little too long,
stuffed her phone number into my back pocket,
I am not sad or depressed
for I will be in Wyoming soon
ready to hike the Absarokas.

The pilot announces
we need to land at Denver.
A price hike for carry-on baggage
has caused a riot in Cheyenne
and spread to airports throughout Wyoming.

In addition, our luggage might have been diverted
to Yakutsk, Siberia.

Waterfalls at 30,000 Feet

It's hard to stand and concentrate
in an airplane bathroom
when the turbulence is heavy,
even though water from the last passenger
sloshes in the sink
and the aluminum bowl
looks like it can take
far more than I can give.

I turn my head
look at myself in the mirror
the skin bubbles under my eyes
the rapier slashes on my forehead.
This is what four hours sleep
two hours in line for baggage check
can do to a man no longer young.
I close my eyes and wonder
if the places I will hike have waterfalls
high
roaring
rushing waterfalls.

The plane hits an air pocket.
My left frontal lobe bounces off the wall
and for a moment
I am in the Mile High Club
fending off a ravenous blonde.

Stalled on the Tarmac

We have sat idle on this plane
for the last half hour
dim lights
air conditioning off
listening to metal banging on metal
as a maintenance crew
tries to open the cabin door.

Passengers curse and cough sporadically.
A flight attendant assures us
they will open the doors shortly
so we can disembark.

In the row behind me,
two elderly women
talk about their sex lives
how easy it is to get it
at their retirement community,
easier than when
the boys came home from Korea.

An overweight man
in a crumpled business suit
snores next to me.
His head flops onto my shoulder
as he puts his hand on my thigh
calls me Gladys
tells me I look beautiful.

I push his hand away
inform him that Gladys left him
for a thinner man.

He continues to snore while I lament
this was the first person
to touch me intimately
in well over a year.

Penicillin and a Romance Novel

Two twenty-somethings
are sitting next to me
in a passenger lounge
at the Denver Airport.
The guy tells his girlfriend
his friend's bachelor party in Rio
will only last a week.
Even the sexiest strippers
won't make him stray again.
She sighs with relief
thankful she did not laser off
the tattoo of his name
on the inside of her thigh
the last time he cheated,
assures him she will consider
his proposal for a polyamorous relationship
but her closest friends are off limits.

While he nods enthusiastically
the overweight woman across from us
bites her lip as she reads a romance novel.
I think this is the one about
a sado-masochistic rich guy
who makes sweet love
to female hardware store workers
after he punches them in the face.
Her purse is on her husband's lap.
He is looking into the open pocket
studying what's inside,
maybe trying to figure out
what happened to his lost virility.

The young couple stands.
As she hugs him tightly
a bottle of penicillin
falls out of his pocket.
When she leaves for her own gate,
I hand it back to him
tell him he might need it.

Betty Grable was Probably Here

We stand in line
ready to board our flight
heads bowed over smart phones
shuffling silently
like a volunteer chain gang.

The flight representative
scans our boarding passes.
Electronic beeps pierce the drone
of a floor waxer
reminding me of an EKG machine
monitoring a comatose patient.

This is an old plane.
It's easy to tell.
The cockpit door is open.
I can see the pilot checking
an instrument panel
I last saw on a documentary
about B-29 Superfortresses.
There is a large indentation
on the ceiling.
Something big was removed from there
a long time ago.
It may have been the bomb rack.

Taking my seat
I look out of the window
watch a group of mechanics
standing on the wing.
One guy shakes his head.
The other imitates a plane

taking a nose dive.
They all laugh.
A woman three rows in front of me sobs.

They climb off
just before the engines start.
Sparks fly from the far turbine.

Part III: Unconscious in Wyoming

Jackson Hole

Arrival: 11:18 p.m. (MT)

Fifteen hours later

Backstage

Airport employees stand
over open suitcases
going through them
before they are loaded.

A bug-eyed man
turns his head from side to side
sees no one is looking
stuffs a pair of women's underwear
into his pocket.
Another man in a baseball cap
is on the phone with his sister.
He asks if Uncle Sid would like
an electric razor for his birthday.
Nodding his acknowledgment
he takes one from a grooming kit
puts it into a paper bag with his name.

The supervisor walks in
asks for everyone's attention
tells his crew
the airline has been getting complaints
from passengers about missing items.
He warns there will be serious consequences
for any employee caught stealing.
Walking up to a suitcase
he takes out a satin nightgown
unfolds it fully.
Hey Stanley!
Looks like your wife decided
to leave you after all.
What's the new guy's name?

Laughter explodes in the cavernous room.
The metal walls vibrate.
Stanley zips up a large duffel bag
muttering angrily under his breath.

Nostalgia in Baggage Claim

The conveyor belt jolts before it starts
rolls around slowly in a circle
like a man with dementia
riding an electric wheelchair.

The microbes of 62 people
and rarely cleaned airplane upholstery
float through my nose and lungs,
fireflies with shredded wings
looking for a place to die.

My luggage comes in view
a brown canvas duffel bag
lined with leather
stitched with parachute cord.
An ex-girlfriend gave it to me
two Christmases ago.
She said it was like our relationship:
you could kick it around
but it would last forever.

I remember how her smile melted
right after she said this
a self-consciousness that worried me
before the next gift
tossed concern from my mind.

The duffel bag passes out of reach
just as my daydream ends.
At first, I feel the urge to go after it
but I'm too tired to slither through the crowd
and I'll get another chance
if I stand here long enough.

The Road to Dubois

The route is black at night:
Jackson Hole Airport to Dubois
an endless necrotic vein
illuminated by the headlights
of an old Suburban truck.

Gnarled and steel-jawed
60-years under a western sun,
my taxi driver fiddles with the GPS.
He's taking me to a ranch
just outside of town
but he doesn't know where it is.
The dispatcher isn't responding.

I ask him about Dubois
to take my mind off the 80-mile trip
the lit engine light
the dial of the gas gauge
creeping to the E.

He corrects my pronunciation:
We say the name the way it's spelled.
The town puts on a rodeo every Friday night.
You and your hiking group should come by.
My niece is singing the National Anthem this week.

Watching the moonscape
along the highway's edge
I call my mother
who still needs reassurance
her 44-year-old boy is okay
an ancient worry

like a tumor made of granite
benign but inoperable.

An hour after midnight
my taxi driver and I
finally arrive at the ranch
where my hiking group is staying
walk a nearly black path
trying to find my cabin.

Stumbling from the weight of my luggage
I try to converse with my driver
compliment his nickel-plated Beretta
glowing like a star
in the beam of my flashlight.
He says he can shoot
fifteen tourists without reloading.

I grow uneasy from the sound of his laughter
hear the growl of a double bass choir
music for a horror movie
imagine a pointless run
through spider-leg branches
a twist of the ankle
followed by maniacal taunting
and the crack of a pistol shot.
(Two years later, my leaf-covered skeleton
flashes on the local news.
An ex-girlfriend points at the TV
laughs with a mouthful of potato chips.)

We round a bend on the path

see a cabin window glowing orange.
A silhouette at the door waves.
My group leader greets me
with a barely stifled yawn.
Fears of murder turn to jubilation.
I give my driver a fifty-dollar tip
and thank him for not killing me.

My Bunkmate Gets Night Terrors

The group leader shows me to my room
informs me breakfast is at 7:00.
Tomorrow will be an easy day.
The first mountain we will hike is only 10000 feet.

A bearded guy in his 50's
reads a comic book on one of the beds.
His name is Bill.
He's a computer programmer
new to hiking
lives with his mom in Scranton.

He asks if I hike much
and whether I'm married.
I reply that I hike more than I date
and get far more satisfaction from the former.
Laughing more than he should
Bill lies on his side
asks if we can leave the light on.
He doesn't like the dark.
Plopping down on my bed
I tell him I am so tired
I could sleep through the Battle of Stalingrad.

Again, Bill laughs more than necessary
warns that he has a tendency to snore
and talk in his sleep
but his night terrors
usually don't bother him.
He hasn't screamed in months.

First Night at the *Absaroka Ranch*

I lie in half sleep
a patient in a dentist's chair
who feels the grip of metal on his tooth
but not the pain of the extraction.

Breathing is hard.
Wyoming air is different
from the strip mall suburbs
of central New Jersey:
thinner
less asbestos and mercury
but cows and horses
bring out the methane.
Car exhaust struggles to stay in my lungs
but gradually evacuates the sub-basement.

The sky is scattered with stars
diamonds in the black gloved hand
of a TV movie cat burglar.
There isn't a streetlight or multi-story building
for over twenty miles.

I dream of a fully loaded tractor trailer
skidding on the Turnpike
during a winter storm
and awaken to the howling of a wolf.

Getting Acquainted Before Breakfast

We mill around the dining room
an abstract painting of names and regional accents.
I introduce myself reluctantly
try to engage in small talk.

Ira tells me he's a *caaah* salesman,
definitely from Massachusetts.
Jim is a retiree from Florida.
When I tell him the *cawfee* is being served,
he laughs
says I must be from New York or New Jersey
adds that he was born in Camden.
I almost give him my condolences.

Virginia is from Ohio.
Clarence likes to be called Duke.
Marty's Korean name is So-Yung Ma.
Tina and Tom finish each other's sentences.
They have three children back in Tennessee:
Teddy
Tucker
and Terrence
and I know from the first moment
of our conversation
I will be avoiding them both.

Ed from Kentucky
comes back from a walk
says there's a *crick* full of fish
just beyond the cow fence.
No one knows what the hell he means.

Unconscious in Wyoming

Gasping and panting
soaked in sheets of sweat
I climb a mountain trail.
Everyone in my hiking group
is already at the summit
except for me and a trail guide
who clicks the hammer of his Colt Revolver
trying to scare me onwards.

I thought a trip to the West would be fun
get away from traffic and noise
demanding nineteen-year-old students
who think an academic advisor is a private butler.
Evening walks in the park
failed to prepare me.

My hiking pole bends in half and I fall
hit my head on a rock.
Visions begin to appear:
A Crow Medicine Man officiates at my funeral,
refers to me by my Indian name,
Idiot Who Chose The Wrong Vacation.
Students gather around my open casket
ask if they can switch their major
appeal their dismissal
declare a leave of absence.
Some hold out phones
tell me their parents want to complain
my death has been a terrible inconvenience.
They want to speak to my supervisor.

The guide kicks my boot

spits a mouthful of water on my forehead
says his ninety-year-old grandmother
can hike up this trail.
Staggering to my feet
I admit to myself
this is still better than being at work.

Return from Death's Balcony

Two ranch hands
drag me to my cabin
throw me on the bed.
The quilt soaks up the dirt and sweat
as I turn over on my back:
a beached salmon
in the final throes of death.

I survived the hike up Death's Balcony
fainted from exhaustion once
but made it to the peak
threw up and then passed out.
I did not regain consciousness
until we got back to the ranch.

One of them puts a wreath of flowers
on the other bed
notices my expression.
Your bunkmate didn't make it.
Didn't bring enough water
got delirious
and took a header off of Cheyenne Ridge.
We already boxed his stuff.
Your group leader is calling
his next of kin.

The matter-of-fact attitude
makes my sweat cold.
Maybe cowboys don't mind death.
Maybe he's a sociopath
working on this ranch
after serving 20 years for manslaughter.

Tomorrow, your group hikes our highest peak:
Suicide Leap.
Bring at least two quarts of water.
Wouldn't want to lose you, too.

The Jackalope

The ranch where we are staying
is similar to most stereotypes.
There is a horse corral and barn.
Cows graze in the fields.
A large house sits on a hill.
The owner's family lives there.

Near an unpaved parking lot,
a wooden bridge spans a tiny stream.
Still limping from this afternoon's hike,
I follow a gravel path
to our group's living area.

A ring of trees encloses a grassy field.
Cabins sit widely spaced along the edge.
In the center of the field is a fire pit
encircled by a ring of chairs and benches.
If Dante sold houses or insurance
this would be his *Inferno*.

This evening is supposed to be cool
so the ranch owner makes a fire
sits on a stool and tells us a story
about a creature called a jackalope
that lives in the mountains.
It is a giant jackrabbit with antelope horns
eats everything from lizards to people
has superhuman strength
the speed of a greyhound.
One attacked him ten years ago
bit off two of his fingers.
He shot it six times but it didn't die.

Some nights, he hears it shrieking in the distance.
Holding up his left hand
we see his ring and pinky fingers are missing.

The group is completely silent.
I then mention I have dated
creatures far more vicious.
No one makes a comment.
They must not like my humor.

Lake Louise

The slope we hike is steep
with powdery soil
that needs a slow, committed patience
I never really learned.

Someone below me starts to slide,
lets out a surprised half-yell
catches himself and laughs.
The people near him laugh
and I smile, too
assured he didn't break his neck.

Pocket knife pain stabs me randomly:
sweat saturated scratches,
a nagging blister
on the ball of my right foot.
Arthritis in my left knee
tells me he'll be visiting more often
once I reach my 50's.

I still don't know why
people do things like this,
exhaust and injure themselves
during the few precious days
they get off from work.
In five more days, I will be home.
My Nissan Sentra
will then get me where I need to go.

The trail finally levels off
and we can see our destination
less than a mile away:

a beautiful purple lake
that flickers in the sunlight.
The sight distracts me from my pain.
My inner voice stops complaining
as my heart continues to thud
like a crate of grenades
exploding underwater.

Majestic and Post-Apocalyptic

I am covered with dust,
an ancient desert statue,
dousing my hand in a rushing stream.

The water is clear enough
to see red spider-web strands
pour from a gash in my finger,
cut trying to slink through a barbed wire fence.

Two antelopes take turns watching me
while the other grazes.
Our trail guide calls them pronghorns
and I admire the way
they look out for each other
waiting for their chance to drink.

This is a strange country,
a scene from an episode of *Star Trek*:
Bright green grass and wildflowers
hug the sides of the water,
beyond that, crumbling mountains
bones and petrified wood.
Nothing that dies here disappears.
It just lies in the sun and bakes.

If majestic and post-apocalyptic
could share the same description
it would be this place
and the silence makes me wish
I didn't have tinnitus
from years of playing Beethoven loudly
to drown out the cacophony
of the congested world around me.

The National Anthem Soars in Dubois

We pile into two trucks
and drive to the Dubois Rodeo,
a local event held every Friday evening.

Climbing the bleachers is harder than usual.
Today's hike through Satan's Staircase
left most of us exhausted
but no one died and even for me
the going felt a little easier.

A pig-tailed girl in her late teens
climbs on the stage.
We groan as we stand
joints crackling in unison.

She begins to sing the National Anthem
and I know right away
this is not going to go well.
As her voice soars,
I imagine bombs bursting in air
to drown out the cries
of the half-cat, half-monkey
being slowly crushed by a steamroller,
but she gets all the words right
so we clap for her courage
and the very brief moment
of national unity.

I sit down
catch the eye of the taxi driver
who brought me to the ranch.
He recognizes me and smiles

his Beretta ready in its holster.
Making a gun
with this thumb and forefinger
he pretends to shoot me and laughs.

The Calf Roper

The steer bursts out of confinement
when they open the gate
and she follows closely behind
on a charging black mare
screaming like a Viking berserker.

Her muscular thighs grip
the sides of the saddle
as she swings a lasso over her head.
Her hat falls off
hastily pinned hair unravels
reveals a light brown industrial fire
raging through a hurricane.

Who is this Absarokan sunflower,
tall and white-skinned
a perfect blend of 19th century cowgirl
and 21st century UFC fighter?
I see the other men look at her,
camouflage baseball caps turned backwards
squeezing beer and soda cans tightly with desire
while their girlfriends check pink-colored phones.
These local boys can't give you what I can:
a cultured man with cosmopolitan sophistication.
Teach me how to ride a horse.
I'll teach you how to jump the turnstile
of a New York City subway
without getting arrested.

The rope falls around the steer's neck
with practiced precision.
She jumps from the horse

wrestles the animal to the ground
straddles him
ties his legs together.
I clap enthusiastically.

The Hike to Austin Peak

The tundra meadow is vast
surrounded by mountains
that see me for what I truly am:
a small, bipedal animal
with only one machine for comfort,
my wristwatch
a reminder
that though I am not time's slave here
I will always be its house husband
roast in the oven every Sunday afternoon.

My lungs no longer hurt when I breathe.
Knees and lower back remind me
that well-preserved middle age
is still no substitute for youth
but I do not care at this altitude.
Birds of prey circle overhead.
I tell them telepathically
there is no death in me now
but if they are patient
I'll be back at work next week.

The people with me are acquaintances.
My family and friends are a country away
but I do not feel alone.
Loneliness
like the ghost of a four-year-old
that hangs from my clavicles
and kicks my stomach
nearly every moment of my waking life
dissipates for a few hours.
The closest thing to peace
settles into me
awkwardly but strongly.

Part IV: The Garden State Beckons

The Garden State Beckons

Today's hike was almost easy:
seven miles at 9000 feet.
We marched through Cowboy's Coffin
like commandos on a mission,
not a stumble, grunt, or gasp between us.
Tonight's dinner has inspired me
to find a place near home
that serves grilled elk.

We've been at the ranch for over a week.
Tonight is our last night here.
I am enjoying myself
until someone mentions air travel.
Then I remember one winter morning
when I was twelve-years-old.
My uncle woke me from a sound sleep
by shaking my foot
with his frozen corpse hand.

This time tomorrow
I will be in New Jersey,
my ant-covered cupcake of a town,
back to bills and traffic
dirty air and angry people
and like the best of my failed relationships
I want to stay a little longer
even though it's time to leave.

The Ride Back to Jackson Hole Airport

The mountains are almost purple
in the soft red light of 5:30 AM.
My taxi driver asks me about my job.
I answer him cordially
but focus more on the passing scenery.

Tires on asphalt lull me into a trance.
I think about what this place was like
a hundred twenty years ago
before skiing became popular
when horseback riding was a necessity
and hiking was simply
putting one foot in front of the other.
Did the people who lived here
ever get used to those mountains?
Did familiarity ever dull the awe?

A siren shriek jolts me back to 2016.
Fire engines race past our SUV
toward a pillar of black smoke
that becomes denser with every mile.
My taxi driver turns on the radio.
We hear the panicked voice of a young newswoman:

The Jackson Hole Airport
has become a scene of chaos.
Enraged passengers
set an A320 Airbus on fire.
United American Continental Airline's
decision to discontinue complimentary almonds
is reported to be the cause.
Domestic flights will proceed as scheduled.
Back to you, Aldo.

Reflections on Absaroka

It is a jigsaw puzzle of beauty and desolation:
sagebrush thriving in parched soil
rocks and bones of many sizes
littering the ground
rivers winding like snakes
through patches of yellow-dappled green
gray mountains partially obscured
by smoldering forest fires.

Absaroka saw disasters:
drought, conflagration, extinction,
long before humans crossed the Bering ice,
endured each one with stoic patience.
It taught me a little of this
and I hope I don't forget.

If Armageddon should ever come
and glass, steel, and asphalt liquefy
pour into the Delaware River
light the Atlantic Ocean on fire,
I doubt things will change here very much.
The Horsemen might just pass it by
having already visited so many times before.

Just Outside the Robot's Maw

I stand at the entrance
to the Jackson Hole airport
not wanting to go in,
watching the electric doors
open and close
like the jaws of a giant robot.

The screech of jet engines
reminds me of home
but I am still yearning
for the mountains
and the forests
the meadows and streams,
places that do not know
urgency or dread.

My mother calls,
asks me if I enjoyed the hiking.
I tell her it was hard
but well worth the effort.
Next year, I'll try to find
another place like this.
Maybe within driving distance.

About the Author

John David Muth is a lifelong resident of central New Jersey. He attended Rutgers University and joined the staff as an academic advisor shortly after graduating. When not working or writing, he enjoys hiking, horseback riding, volunteering for environmental causes, and traveling. Much of his poetry satirizes romantic relationships, modern culture, technology, and higher education. He is a member of the U.S. 1 Poet's Cooperative. His work has appeared in such journals as *Anti-Heroin Chic, Verse-Virtual, San Pedro River Review,* and *U.S. 1 Worksheets.* He is the author of two collections of poetry: *A Love for Lavender Dragons* (Aldrich Press, 2016) and *Inevitable Carbon* (Aldrich Press, 2017).

www.ingramcontent.com/pod-product-compliance
Lightning Source LLC
LaVergne TN
LVHW051606080426
835510LV00020B/3162